JAZZ Standards for Vocalists
with Combo Accompaniment

A collection of 10 songs
Arranged by Dave Wolpe

AF822315

CONTENTS – Vocalist

INSTRUMENTATION

Vocalist—(29938)
B♭ Trumpet—(29939)
E♭ Alto Saxophone—(29940)
B♭ Tenor Saxophone—(29941)
Trombone—(29942)
E♭ Baritone Saxophone (Optional Part)—(29943)
Guitar—(29944)
Bass—(29945)
Drumset—(29946)
Piano/Conductor—(29947)

Complete Set—(29948)

Alfred

Alfred Publishing Co., Inc.
16320 Roscoe Blvd., Suite 100
P.O. Box 10003
Van Nuys, CA 91410-0003
alfred.com

ISBN-10: 0-7390-5244-6
ISBN-13: 978-0-7390-5244-0

I'VE GOT YOU UNDER MY SKIN

VOCAL SOLO

Words and Music by
COLE PORTER
Arranged by DAVE WOLPE

MODERATE SWING (♩ = 132)
I've got you under my skin. I've got you deep in the heart of me.
So deep in my heart, you're really a part of me.
I've got you under my skin.
I tried so not to give in.
I said to myself, "This affair never will go so well."
But why should I try to resist when, darling, I know so well,
I've got you under my skin.
I'd

sac - ri - fice an - y - thing, come what might, for the sake of hav - ing you
near. In spite of a warn - ing voice that comes in the night and re -
peats and re - peats in my ear: "Don't you know, lit - tle fool,
you ne - ver can win. Use your men - tal - i - ty.
Wake up to re - al - i - ty." But each
time I do, just the thought of you makes me stop, be - fore I be -
TO CODA
gin, 'cause I've got you under my
skin.
D.S. AL CODA
I'd
CODA
skin. 'cause I've got you
un - der my skin.

SUMMER WIND

VOCAL SOLO

English Words by JOHNNY MERCER
Original German Lyrics by HANS BRADTKE
Music by HENRY MAYER
Arranged by DAVE WOLPE

MODERATE SWING (♩ = 106)
The sum - mer wind came blow - ing in a - cross the sea, it lin - gered there to touch your hair and walk with me. All sum - mer long we sang a song and strolled the gold - en sand, two sweet - hearts and the sum - mer wind.
Like pain - ted kites, the days and nights went fly - ing by, the world was new be - neath a blue um - brel - la sky. Then soft - er than a pip - er man one day it called to you.

I lost you to the sum - mer wind.
39
8
47
7
The
55
au - tumn wind, the win - ter winds have come and gone,
and still the days, the one - ly days go
on and on.
And guess who sighs his
lull - a - bies through nights that nev - er end,
my fick - le friend, the sum - mer wind.
My fick - le friend, the sum - mer wind, the
sum - mer wind,
the sum - mer wind.

THEY CAN'T TAKE THAT AWAY FROM ME

VOCAL SOLO

Music and Lyrics by
GEORGE GERSHWIN
and IRA GERSHWIN
Arranged by DAVE WOLPE

MODERATE SWING (♩ = 116)
3
The way you wear your hat,
6
the way you sip your tea,
the way you sing off key,
the mem - r'y of all that,
the way you haunt my dreams,
no, no! They
1.
can't take that a - way from me! The way your smile just beams,
2.
can't take that a - way from me!
16
We may nev - er, nev - er
meet a - gain on the bump - y road to love. Still I'll
al - ways, al - ways keep the mem - r'y of

24
the way you hold your knife,
the way we danced till three,
the way you've changed my life,
TO CODA
no, no! They can't take that a - way from me! No, they
can't take that a - way from me!
36
8
44
7
D.S. 𝄋 AL CODA
We may nev-
CODA
can't take that a - way, they can't take that a - way,
no, they can't take that a - way from me!

HOW HIGH THE MOON

VOCAL SOLO

Words by NANCY HAMILTON
Music by MORGAN LEWIS
Arranged by DAVE WOLPE

33
TO CODA
night would shine if you would come to me soon. Un - til you
will, how still my heart, how high the moon!
41
16
57
16
73
7
D.S. % AL CODA
There is no
CODA
will, how still my heart
Un - til you will, how still my heart, how high the moon!
How high the moon!

MY FUNNY VALENTINE

VOCAL SOLO

Words by LORENZ HART
Music by RICHARD RODGERS
Arranged by DAVE WOLPE

SLOWLY (♩ = 82)
7
8
My fun - ny val - en - tine, sweet com - ic val - en - tine,
you made me smile with my heart.
Your looks are laugh - a - ble, un - pho - to - graph - a - ble,
yet you're my fav - 'rite work of art. Is your
24
fig - ure less than Greek? Is your mouth a lit - tle weak? When you
o - pen it to speak, are you smart? But

32
don't change a hair for me, not if you care for me.
Stay, lit - tle Val - en - tine, stay.
Each day is Val - en - tine's day.
44
15
Is your
60
fig - ure less than Greek? Is your mouth a lit - tle weak? When you
o - pen it to speak, are you smart? But
68
don't change a hair for me, not if you care for me.
Stay, lit - tle Val - en - tine, stay.
MOLTO RIT.
VERY SLOW
Each day is Val - en - tine's day.

SOMETHING'S GOTTA GIVE

VOCAL SOLO

Words and Music by
JOHNNY MERCER
Arranged by DAVE WOLPE

BRIGHT SWING (♩ = 168)
8
1-8
9
When an ir - re - sis - ti - ble force such as you meets an old im - mov - a - ble ob - ject like me, you can bet as sure as you live,
Some - thing's Got - ta Give, Some - thing's Got - ta Give, Some - thing's Got - ta Give.
25
When an ir - re - pres - si - ble smile such as yours warms an old im - pla - ca - ble heart such as mine,
don't say no, be - cause I in - sist.
41
Some - where, some - how, some - one's got - ta be kissed. So, en - garde,
who knows what the fates have in store,

from their vast my - ste - ri - ous sky? I'll try hard
ig - nor - ing those lips I a - dore,
but how long can an - y - one try?
57
Fight, fight, fight, fight, fight it with all of our might,
chan - ces are some hea - ven - ly star - spang - led night,
To Coda
we'll find out as sure as we live.
Some - thing's Got - ta Give, Some - thing's Got - ta Give, Some - thing's Got - ta
73
16
89
15
D.S. al Coda
Give.
So, en - garde,
Coda
Some - thing's Got - ta Give, Some - thing's Got - ta Give,
Some - thing's Got - ta Give, Some - thing's Got - ta Give,
Some - thing's Got - ta Give. Some - thing's
Got - ta Give. Some - thing's Got - ta Give.

TOO CLOSE FOR COMFORT

VOCAL SOLO

Words and Music by
JERRY BOCK, LARRY HOLOFCENER
and GEORGE DAVID WEISS
Arranged by DAVE WOLPE

MODERATE SWING (♩ = 156)
Be wise,
be smart, be - have my heart, don't up - set your cart when he's so close.
be sweet, but be dis - creet, don't go off your beat. He's too
Be soft,
close for com - fort.
Too close, too close for com - fort, please not a - gain.
Too close, too close to know just when to say, "when."
Be firm, be fair, be sure, be - ware, on your guard. Take care while there's

35
such temp - ta - tion. One thing leads to an - oth - er,
too late to run for cov - er, he's much too
TO CODA
close for com - fort now!
43
1.
2.
53
Too close, too close for com - fort, please not a - gain.
D.S. 𝄋 AL CODA
Too close, too close to know just when to say, "when." Be firm,
CODA
He's much too close for com - fort now! Too close.
Now!

I GET A KICK OUT OF YOU

VOCAL SOLO

Words by Music by
COLE PORTER
Arranged by DAVE WOLPE

MODERATE SWING (♩ = 146)
6
1-6
7
I Get no kick from cham - pagne.
Mere al - co - hol does - n't thrill me at all. So
tell me why should it be true, that
23
I get a kick out of you?
Some like the be - bop re - frain,
I'm sure that if I heard ev - en one riff it would
bore me ter - rif - ic - 'ly too. Yet
39
I get a kick out of you.
I get a kick ev - 'ry time I see you

stand - ing there be - fore me.
I get a kick tho' it's clear to me you
55
ob - vious - ly don't a - dore me.
I get no kick in a plane.
Fly - ing too high with some guy in the sky is my
TO CODA
i - dea of noth - ing to do. Yet
I get a kick out of you.
71
16
87
16
D.S. 𝄋 AL CODA
71-86
87-102
CODA
I get a kick, yes! I get a
kick, yes! I get a kick out of you.

JUST FRIENDS

VOCAL SOLO

Music by JOHN KLENNER
Lyric by SAM M. LEWIS
Arranged by DAVE WOLPE

FAST SWING (𝅗𝅥 = 180)
Just
friends, lov - ers no more. Just
friends, but not like be - fore. To
think of what we've been and not to kiss a - gain
seems like pre - tend - ing it is - n't the
end - ing. Two friends drift - ing a -
part, two friends, but one brok - en
heart. We loved, we laughed, we cried, and

TO CODA
sud - den - ly love died, the sto - ry ends and
we're just friends.
43
8
43-50
51
8
51-58
59
8
59-66
67
7
67-73
D.S. % AL CODA
Just
CODA
we're just friends
We're just friends.

NIGHT AND DAY

VOCAL SOLO

Words by Music by
COLE PORTER
Arranged by DAVE WOLPE

Moderate Swing (♩ = 132)
10
Night and day you are the
one. On - ly you be - neath the moon
and un - der the sun. Wheth - er
near to me or far, it's no mat - ter, dar - ling,
where you are I think of you night and day.
27
Day and night, why is it so,
that this long - ing for you fol - lows wher - ev - er I
go? In the roar - ing traf - fic's boom, in the
si - lence of my lone - ly room I think of you,

night and day. Night and day,
under the hide of me.
There's an oh, such a hungry yearning burning in-
side of me. And it's torment won't be
through 'til you let me spend my life making love to you,
TO CODA
day and night, night and day.
D.S. AL CODA
Night and day
CODA
Night and day